Tell ME What YOU Remember

FAMILY LIFE

Sarah Ridley

W
FRANKLIN WATTS
LONDON • SYDNEY

Franklin Watts
First published in Great Britain in 2015 by
The Watts Publishing Group

Series editor: Sarah Peutrill
Series design: Basement68

The Author and Publisher would
like to thank everyone who has
kindly contributed their photos
and memories to this book.

Dewey classification: 392
HB ISBN: 978 1 4451 3985 2
Library Ebook ISBN: 978 1 4451 4006 3

Printed in China

Franklin Watts
An imprint of
Hachette Children's Group
Part of The Watts Publishing Group
Carmelite House
50 Victoria Embankment
London EC4Y 0DZ

An Hachette UK Company
www.hachette.co.uk

www.franklinwatts.co.uk

Picture credits: Barnaby's Studios
Ltd/Mary Evans PL: 9b. John
Chase/Museum of London: 8t.
Thomas Cook Archive/Mary Evans
PL: 19t. Daily Herald Archives/
Science and Society PL: 12t. Greg
Balfour Evans/Alamy: 16br. John
Gay/Historic England/Mary
Evans PL: 11t. John Gay/ NMR/
Mary Evans PL: 10. Roger Mayne/
Mary Evans PL: 14. Ministry
of Information/IWM: 6, 7b.
Moviestore Collection/Alamy: 13t.
Martin O'Neill/Getty Images: 22.
Retrograph/Mary Evans PL: 11c.
Ken Russell/Topfoto: 9c. Science
Museum/Science and Society PL:
12b. All other photographs are
kindly given by the people who
contributed their memories.

Contents

Family Life

Everybody has different experiences of family life. How do you spend time together? Do you live near to grandparents or cousins? Read on to find out about different experiences of family life in the past.

Jessie, born 1940, remembers...

My father owned a small farm and a flour mill with his brother. My cousins and my granny lived in the same village as we did. I am about ten in this photo taken on a day out at the pier with my family.

Memories are what we remember about the past. Everyone has stories to tell about family life when they were growing up. Talking to people about what they remember can help us to learn about the past.

Simon, born 1963, remembers...

I spent the first ten years of my life in Tanzania. My brothers and I mostly did what we wanted. I didn't go to school until I was seven so Mum taught me to read.

Molly, born 2001, remembers...

My mum is Japanese and my dad is English. I live near my English cousins and grandparents but I only visit my Japanese family every few years. On my last visit, I had great fun with my Japanese cousins, floating down a river.

FIND OUT MORE

Ask your parents and grandparents to tell you about family life when they were children. Do they think your family life is different from theirs?

5

Wartime Families

When war broke out in 1939, families were split apart. Fathers and brothers joined the army, navy or air force, or became air-raid wardens or fire fighters. Some mothers took on jobs in factories or driving buses. In places where air raids were expected, children were evacuated to a safer part of the country.

Between 1–3 September 1939, 1.5 million children were evacuated. By January 1940, half of them had returned home. There were more evacuations during the war. Some families made their own arrangements.

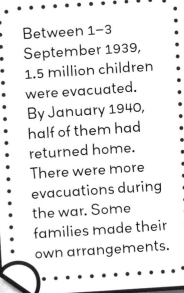

In 1940 these children from Bristol travelled by train to Devon as evacuees. Local families looked after them. While some children enjoyed the experience others were terribly homesick.

Nick, born 1937, remembers...

My father spent most of the war in the army, helping to defend the coast from possible invasion. We only saw him when he was on leave.

My mother took me to Cornwall, away from air raids. After a while we came home to Ipswich and sheltered from air raids in our cellar. From the attic, I saw doodlebugs flying up the River Orwell. They made a stuttering noise until they ran out of fuel – when they dropped like a stone.

A doodlebug (flying bomb) dropped on this London street in 1944, killing people and destroying homes.

Home

Between 1918 and 1939, about four million new homes were built. Sadly, some of these and many others were destroyed by air raids during the Second World War. After the war, the government and building companies started to build houses and flats for people to rent or buy. House building has continued through the decades.

To help provide homes for families after the Second World War, over 150,000 prefabs were built. They were only supposed to last for ten years but some still stand today.

Joan, born 1932, remembers...

Lots of people lived in caravans or prefabs after the war. We moved into our own caravan on our wedding day in 1953. The caravan had electric power but the showers and loos were in a separate building.

We didn't have central heating or an inside loo at home when I was growing up but we did have a television before most people on our street. This photo shows my brother, sister and parents in our backyard in the 1950s.

In 1948 a boat called the Empire Windrush brought about 500 West Indians to Britain to begin new lives. Many other people from Commonwealth countries followed. This photo was taken in 1954 and shows children playing outside their new London home, a big house divided into flats.

This photo was taken in the late 1960s. These children were living on a housing estate.

Housework

In the 1950s, women were expected to give up work when they married. They looked after their children and spent their days cleaning, shopping and cooking. Gradually more families could afford to buy washing machines, fridges and hoovers and these machines saved a lot of time. This helped the growing number of mothers who went out to work from the 1960s onwards.

Barbara, born 1932, remembers...

Monday was washday. My father lit a fire under the boiler and when the water was hot, my mum washed all our clothes and sheets by hand.

Irene, born 1939, remembers...

My mother always found me a job to do if she thought I was about to read a book. She thought that was a waste of time! I'd help out by doing the washing up, like this little girl, and I'd run errands to the shops.

Jane, born 1963, remembers...

Lucky me!

BENDIX *automatically* THE BEST

SOAKS DAMP DRIES WASHES DRAINS RINSES THREE TIMES AND SWITCHES ITSELF OFF

My parents bought a washing machine when they had children. Dad dried up the dishes sometimes but never cleaned or cooked! When we were older, we took it in turns to help Mum.

Tom, born 1987, remembers...

My step-dad ironed his own shirts and fixed things around the house but my mum did most of the housework.

FIND OUT MORE

Make a list of all the machines that help your family do the housework. Ask your grandparents which ones their families owned when they were children.

11

TV and Radio

By the 1940s, almost every family in Britain owned a radio. At 6 o'clock in the evening, families gathered together to listen to the news, followed by comedy, music and drama. It was the Queen's Coronation in 1953 that made many people go out and buy a television. Today most families own radios and televisions, to enjoy together or alone in their bedrooms.

Roger, born 1940, remembers...

I think all of our friends and neighbours had televisions before we did. We had a radio, like this family. After our evening meal all of us listened to the adventures of Dick Barton – Special Agent. He saved the world so many times!

In 1953, 20 million people watched the coronation of Queen Elizabeth II in black and white on a television a bit like this one.

1922 The BBC started radio broadcasts.
1936 The BBC started TV broadcasts.
1950s There were two TV stations – BBC 1 and ITV.
1980s/1990s Many families bought a video recorder.
1990s onwards Many more satellite and digital TV stations.
Late 1990s/2000s People bought DVD players to watch films on their TVs.

Jane, born 1963, remembers...

There was an hour of children's programmes on the TV after school and I enjoyed *The Clangers* and *Blue Peter*. On Saturday mornings we tried to watch *Swap Shop* but Mum thought it was a real waste of time!

Sarah, born 1973, remembers...

I listened to the Top 40 on Radio 1 every Sunday afternoon and taped the songs onto a cassette tape to listen to in the week.

Tom, born 1987, remembers...

My brother and I woke up very early so we would go downstairs to watch cartoons on TV before breakfast.

FIND OUT MORE

Ask you parents and grandparents about the TV and radio programmes they enjoyed when they were children.

Family Time

Ask your parents, grandparents and great-grandparents how they spent time with their families. They will have many different stories to tell, just as people do today. Here are a few memories.

Irene, born 1939, remembers...

My favourite part of the week was going to the pictures on a Saturday afternoon with my brother and sister. We walked to the cinema on our own and queued up like these children. We watched a film, a cartoon and episodes from a serial, such as Batman or Superman.

Jessie, born 1940, remembers...

Sunday was Dad's day off. Mum cooked a roast lunch and then Dad drove us to his farm to see the animals. In the evening, we loved playing games like Monopoly and Snakes and Ladders.

Annie, born 1949, remembers...

My dad owned a car and he took us for picnics by the seaside on summer weekends. I'm about 10 and my brother is six in this photo and we've just flown our kite on the beach.

Yvonne, born 1968, remembers...

I had great fun with my brothers. We spent a lot of time riding our bikes and playing with friends on the streets outside our home.

Birthdays and Christmas

People started singing 'Happy Birthday to You' about a hundred years ago. By then, many of the ways we celebrate Christmas were already popular such as decorating a Christmas tree, giving presents, eating turkey and sending Christmas cards.

Roger, born 1940, remembers...

We didn't celebrate birthdays much at all but Christmas was special. We each had a present an a book, such as a Rupert annual, as well as an apple and an orange.

David, born 1957, remembers ...

This photo was taken in our garden on my sixth birthday. I'm holding my new Etch-A-Sketch and the puppy was a present too.

Yvonne, born 1968, remembers...

We went to church at midnight on Christmas Eve. We ate a dinner with a Caribbean twist – a roast turkey dinner plus hot pepper sauce, yams, plantain, rice and peas. Here's my sister in traditional Caribbean dress in the 1970s.

Liz, born 1979, remembers...

We celebrated Christmas, birthdays and adoption days in my family. Our parents always told us we were adopted so it felt completely normal. On our adoption days, we'd do something special and get a present.

FIND OUT MORE

Ask your parents and grandparents about the best Christmas they ever had. What was special about it?

Family Holidays

Irene, born 1939, remembers...

After the Second World War, many more families could afford a holiday. Most of them spent a week by the sea, staying in a boarding house, a holiday camp or a hotel. In the 1970s cheaper air fares meant that families began taking holidays abroad in France, Spain or Greece. Since the 1990s, travelling by plane has become even easier but many families still prefer a holiday by the sea in Britain.

We usually went to a holiday camp with a big group of friends and relatives. We sent our stuff ahead in a big metal trunk and followed a day or two later by train. We'd go to the beach and take part in contests and games organised by the holiday camp.

Irene

From the late 1950s, holiday companies started to sell package holidays. The cost of the holiday included the flights, hotel and some meals.

Suzanne, born 1966, remembers...

Most of my family holidays were spent by the sea, staying in a caravan or a holiday cottage. We swam every day, built sandcastles and ate picnics even if the weather was cold and grey! As teenagers, we went on canal boat holidays.

Lisbeth, born 1997, remembers...

I was born in Britain but my grandparents live in India. My dad likes to take my brother and me for holidays to the places he enjoyed when he was growing up in India.

Changing Families

After the Second World War, it became much more common for unhappy couples to get divorced. Gradually, from the 1970s onwards, all sorts of families have become normal – families with one parent or two, married parents, unmarried parents or step-parents. Children today often live a long way from grandparents, who sometimes live on the other side of the world.

Roger, born 1940, remembers...

I had seven brothers and sisters. This photo was taken when I was seven with Mick, Sandra and Trevor. When I was growing up I knew other people who had lots of brothers and sisters too. When I married, I only had two children and my own children have also had small families.

Pippa, born 1964, remembers...

When I was ten my parents split up. It felt strange trying to be part of two families. At Christmas my brother and I had to eat two lunches — one with our mother, and one around the corner with our father's new family.

Olivia, born 1999, remembers...

I live in the USA but I visit my grandparents in England every summer. I have nine first cousins and these three are my age.

Esther, born 1974, remembers...

My mum brought me up on her own. At Christmas, my uncle and aunt came over and it was always my job to hand out the presents.

Childhood Bedroom

Ask your parents and grandparents to describe their childhood bedroom. Did they share it with brothers or sisters? How much time did they spend in their room and what did they do there?

Jessie, born 1940, remembers...

I shared a bedroom with my sister. It just had beds, a wardrobe, a chest-of-drawers and a mirror. We never spent much time there as there was nothing to do and it was usually very cold.

This photo was taken in 1977, the year of the Queen's Silver Jubilee. This teenage girl has put up posters and probably listened to a radio or a record player in her room.

Timeline

Use this timeline to see at a glance some of the information in this book.

1922 The British Broadcasting Corporation (BBC) began radio broadcasts.

1920s–30s Four million new homes were built across Britain.

1930s–40s Women tended to have at least two or three children, and sometimes had up to seven or eight.

1930s–60s Thousands of cinemas ran children's film clubs every Saturday.

1936 The BBC began television broadcasts.

1939–45 The Second World War was fought in Europe and around the world.

September 1939 The government organised the evacuation of 1.5 million British children from areas of danger.

1945–early 1950s Over 150,000 prefabs were built as temporary homes.

1948 The boat, the *Empire Windrush*, brought the first wave of West Indian immigrants to live and work in Britain.

1950s Women were expected to stop work when they married.

1953 Queen Elizabeth II's Coronation.

Late 1950s Package holidays began – holidays where the flight and hotel were part of the holiday price.

1960s The BBC launched BBC 2 and began broadcasting programmes in colour.

1960s onwards Washing machines, televisions and other machines became cheaper so more families could afford them. More mothers started to go out to work.

1969 A new law meant that unhappy couples could divorce each other after they had lived separately for two years.

1970s Cheaper air fares made package holidays abroad much more popular with families.

1970s onwards Women often chose to have two children rather than big families, or chose to remain childless.

1977 Queen Elizabeth II's Silver Jubilee.

1982 Channel 4 TV station began broadcasts.

1990s onwards Many more digital and satellite television channels were available. Air fares became even cheaper and local airports expanded. Many families owned more than one television as well as a computer.

Glossary

air raid An attack by aircraft dropping bombs. Air-raid wardens helped people find the nearest shelter.

boarding house A large house where visitors could rent a room and receive some meals from a landlady or landlord.

boiler A large metal tank for heating water.

broadcast Another name for a radio or television programme.

Commonwealth, the An organisation made up of the United Kingdom and 52 other countries, many of which were once part of the British Empire.

coronation The ceremony when a king or queen is crowned.

decade A period of ten years.

doodlebug The nickname for the German V1 flying bomb.

Etch-A-Sketch A drawing toy that became very popular in the 1960s.

evacuee Children became evacuees during the Second World War (1939–45) when they were moved – evacuated – from places where air raids were expected to safer areas of the country.

holiday camp Holiday camps had chalets for families to stay in, a swimming pool and lots of entertainments.

pier A long walkway stretching into the sea.

prefab A prefabricated building. Large sections of the building are made in a factory and then put together where required.

Silver Jubilee In 1977, the people of the United Kingdom celebrated the fact that Queen Elizabeth II had been on the throne for 25 years.

Top 40 The 40 most popular songs at any one time.

West Indies The islands of the Bahamas, Jamaica, Trinidad and Tobago make up the British West Indies.

Index